First Picture Dictionary
Animals

Primo dizionario illustrato
Animali

Pig
Maiale

Butterfly
Farfalla

Rabbit
Coniglio

Fox
Volpe

Illustrated by Anna Ivanir

www.kidkiddos.com
Copyright ©2025 by KidKiddos Books Ltd.
support@kidkiddos.com

All rights reserved. No part of this book may be reproduced in any form or by any electronic or mechanical means, including information storage and retrieval systems, without written permission from the publisher, except in the case of a reviewer, who may quote brief passages embodied in critical articles or in a review.
First edition, 2025

Library and Archives Canada Cataloguing in Publication
First Picture Dictionary – Animals (English Italian Bilingual edition)
ISBN: 978-1-83416-285-0 paperback
ISBN: 978-1-83416-286-7 hardcover
ISBN: 978-1-83416-284-3 eBook

Wild Animals
Animali selvatici

Lion
Leone

Tiger
Tigre

Giraffe
Giraffa

✦ *A giraffe is the tallest animal on land.*
✦ *La giraffa è l'animale terrestre più alto.*

Elephant
Elefante

Monkey
Scimmia

Wild Animals
Animali selvatici

Hippopotamus
Ippopotamo

Panda
Panda

Fox
Volpe

Rhino
Rinoceronte

Deer
Cervo

Moose
Alce

Wolf
Lupo

✦ A moose is a great swimmer and can dive underwater to eat plants!
✦ *L'alce è un ottimo nuotatore e può immergersi per mangiare piante!*

Squirrel
Scoiattolo

Koala
Koala

✦ A squirrel hides nuts for winter, but sometimes forgets where it put them!
✦ *Lo scoiattolo nasconde le noci per l'inverno, ma a volte dimentica dove le ha messe!*

Gorilla
Gorilla

Pets
Animali domestici

Canary
Canarino

✦ A frog can breathe through its skin as well as its lungs!
✦ *La rana può respirare sia attraverso la pelle che con i polmoni!*

Guinea Pig
Porcellino d'India

Frog
Rana

Hamster
Criceto

Goldfish
Pesce rosso

Dog
Cane

✦ *Some parrots can copy words and even laugh like a human!*
✦ *Alcuni pappagalli possono imitare le parole e perfino ridere come un essere umano!*

Cat
Gatto

Parrot
Pappagallo

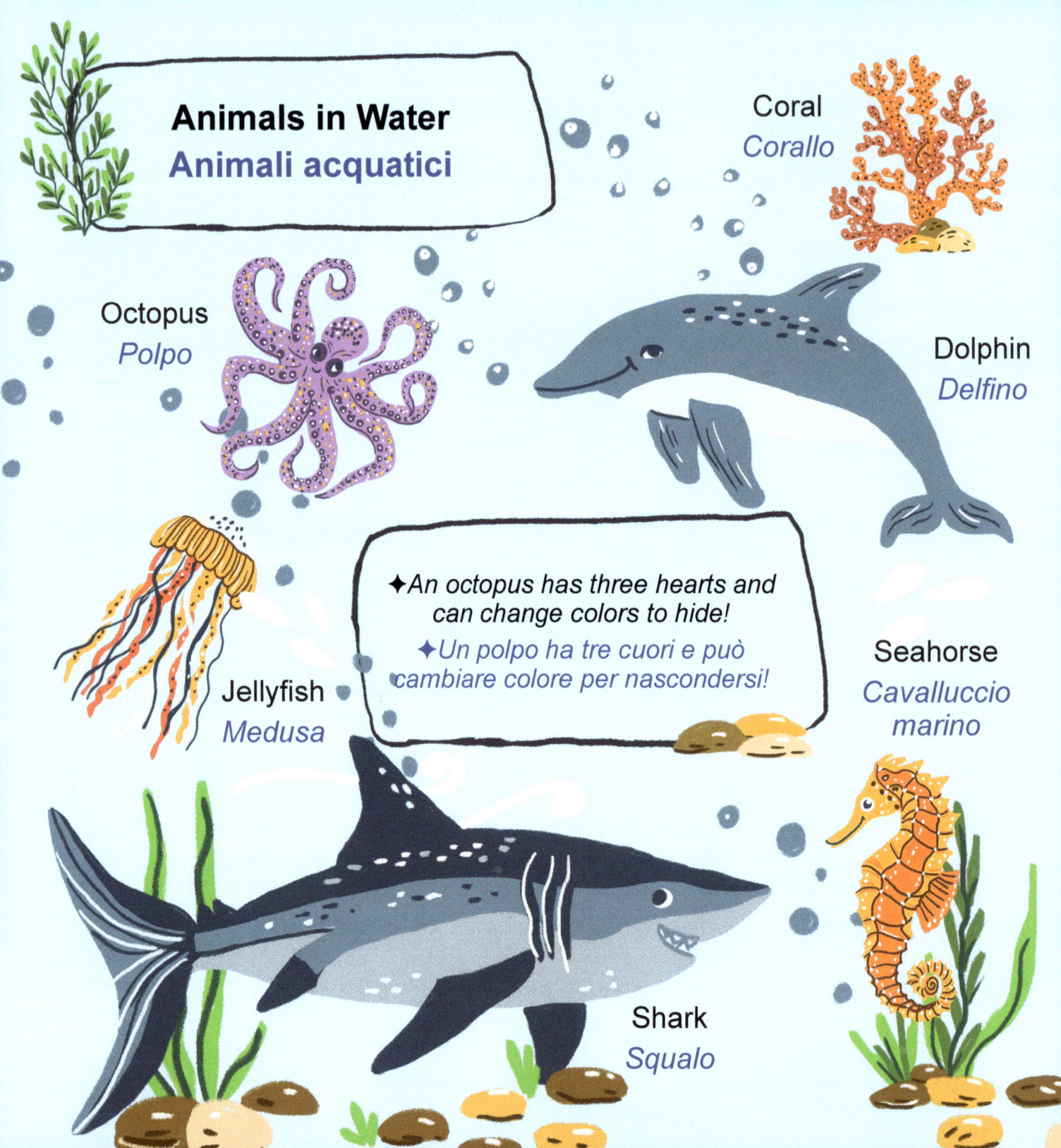

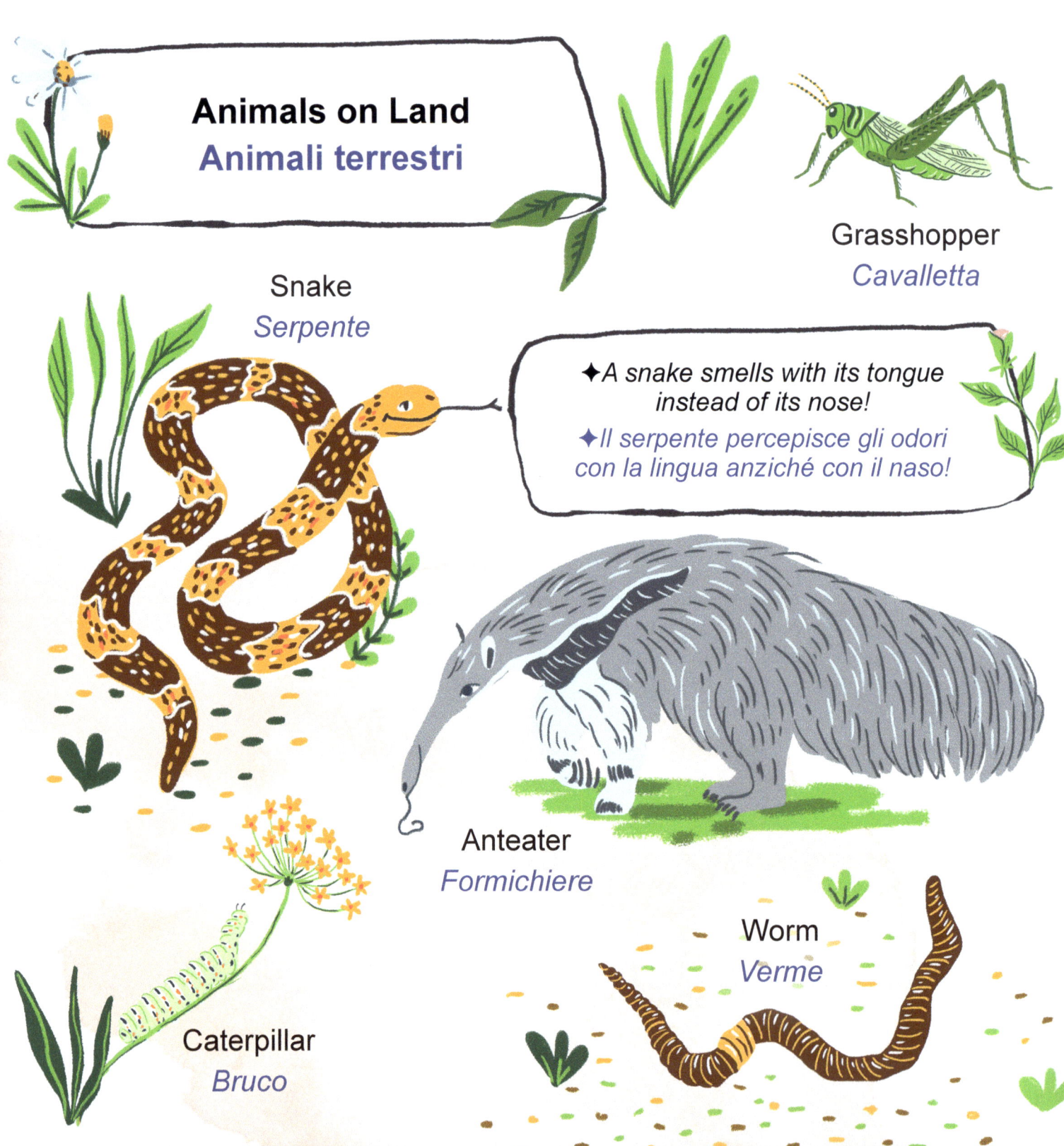

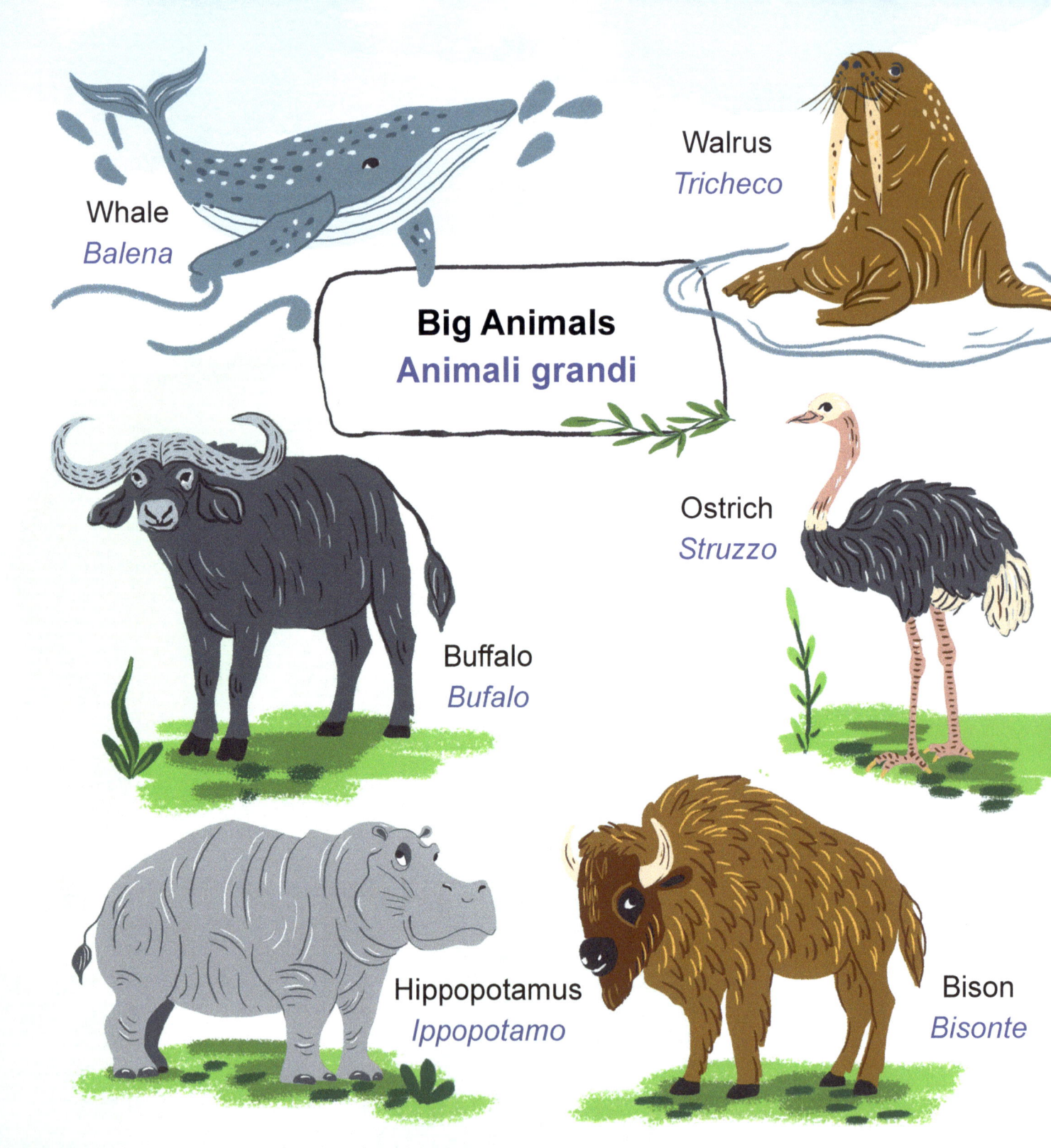

Small Animals
Animali piccoli

Chameleon
Camaleonte

Spider
Ragno

✦ An ostrich is the biggest bird, but it cannot fly!
  ✦ *Lo struzzo è l'uccello più grande, ma non può volare!*

Bee
Ape

✦ A snail carries its home on its back and moves very slowly.
  ✦ *La lumaca porta la sua casa sulla schiena e si muove molto lentamente.*

Snail
Lumaca

Mouse
Topo

Quiet Animals
Animali silenziosi

Turtle
Tartaruga

Ladybug
Coccinella

✦ A turtle can live both on land and in water.
✦ *La tartaruga può vivere sia sulla terra che in acqua.*

Fish
Pesce

Lizard
Lucertola

Owl
Gufo

Bat
Pipistrello

✦An owl hunts at night and uses its hearing to find food!
✦*Il gufo caccia di notte e usa il suo udito per trovare il cibo!*

✦A firefly glows at night to find other fireflies.
✦*La lucciola si illumina di notte per trovare altre lucciole.*

Raccoon
Procione

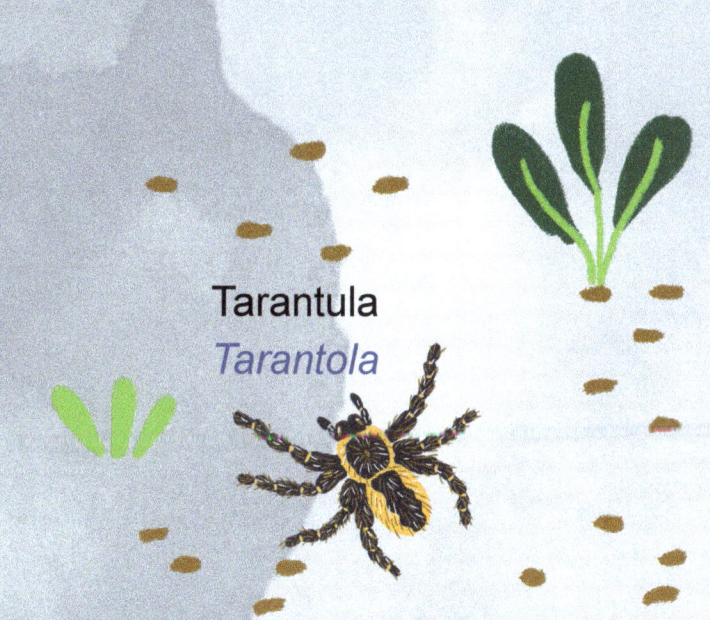

Tarantula
Tarantola

Colorful Animals
Animali colorati

A flamingo is pink
Il fenicottero è rosa

An owl is brown
Il gufo è marrone

A swan is white
Il cigno è bianco

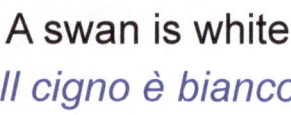

An octopus is purple
Il polpo è viola

A frog is green
La rana è verde

✦ A frog is green, so it can hide among the leaves.
✦ *La rana è verde, così può nascondersi tra le foglie.*

Animals and Their Babies
Animali e i loro piccoli

Cow and Calf
Mucca e Vitello

Cat and Kitten
Gatto e Gattino

✦ *A chick talks to its mother even before it hatches.*
✦ *Il pulcino parla con sua madre ancora prima di nascere.*

Chicken and Chick
Gallina e Pulcino

Dog and Puppy
Cane e Cucciolo

Butterfly and Caterpillar
Farfalla e Bruco

Sheep and Lamb
Pecora e Agnello

Horse and Foal
Cavallo e Puledro

Pig and Piglet
Maiale e Maialino

Goat and Kid
Capra e Capretto